The Seasons of Words

Katie Donovan

2

Incarnate Press

an Imprint of Incarnate Press, LLC

Published by Incarnate Press, LLC

Incarnate Press and the colophon are trademarks of Incarnate Press, LLC.

First Edition 2015

Paperback ISBN: 978-0-9889424-2-4

EBook ISBN: 978-0-9889424-3-1

Table of Contents

8

Winter

In the winter moments of life we experience longing, loss, and loneliness.

It is a time of intense emotions that fill up our lives and seems to never end.

Yet within it we also find solace, peace, and quiet reflection.

"The First Goodbye"

It was like the rain pounding against my soul.
It was like clouds coveting my only sunshine,
As the wind ripped at my tears and stole my words
That were laced with grief.
And I stared at the vast emptiness of black sky
Filled with silence
That was all I was left with.

"Enduring Love?"
Folded and creased like an ironed shirt,
Stuck in a back closet,
Taken out when needed,

That's how he treats me now.

Yet his words are like honey,
And his movements smooth as butter,
And I believe him.

Then the silence settles.

I am a mouse on a wheel
Striving for nothing,
But believing in something.

And so I wait.

I've bottled my words in a jar, gave them to him.
Now they've sunk like stones to the bottom,
And he carries on.

My jar of hope in the closet collects dust.
He flies from one thing to another too busy to
remember me,
But armed with an excuse to sting.

I am a flower wilting.

"Slide into dreams"
As I slide into bed
Beneath a familiar fluffy comfort
I feel like a vine
Split in many directions.

This vine:
I am solid marble
With gray and blue swirls
And I remember the woman
In the mirror
Who used to dream,
And I am inspired by her passion, her drive.
I sink into her moment
When she used to cup words in her hands
And blow them onto a page,
When she was a glossy maple
And her arms could reach forever.

A different vine:
Silver linings are pinned to the ground
And dreams drift like smoke.
I can't grab them,
Only watch them pass.
I see the sun through filtered glass,
A distorted glow of what could be,
A twisted yellow I had imagined would shine
full and bright.

The last vine:
He's there holding our memories
And I smile sadly.
He holds my dreams without a future,
Dreams frayed at the ends.
Somewhere the cracks on our path
Turned to crevices and divides.
Us could turn to a solitary I
Because we can't see the way.
I wish someone would turn on a light.
We stumble in the dark.

I thought I was fulfilling the desires of my heart,
Only to find a tease, a taste of something truly
beautiful.
I thought I was melting into something
that would harden to gold.
I thought I was losing myself into something where
I would find more of me,
Only to find I could lose more.

If all we'll ever have are memories,
And I'm left with me
Where do I turn to find who I've lost in blended
moments?

"Never Dreaming"
Flung to the bed
By the pull of sleep

I curl into his embrace,
Wait 'til he slides into slumber.

I sigh.
I cling to our memories,
      When we were fire on the dance floor,
      When his touch singed my skin,
      And his voice was as smooth as water.

Somehow he became full of cotton.
The anchor I clung to, now molten metal.

He swallows stones
With a bleary look in his eyes.

He wanders in circles,
Unsure which way to go.

I string words and end up tying him in knots.
Each conversation I cut one away.

Soon I will cut myself out of the picture
I painted of our life,

If he doesn't become clear as glass,
And as certain as steel that he wants a future with me
      And is willing to walk on nails for it.

"Us"

I taste the dust of my dreams,
Gritty and sharp.

My home,
Fragments of photos and memories,
Full of color and movement.

I sit and wait
For nothing.

I am a fool
To cling to a broken dream.

Our love was like a stained glass window
Now the glass is shattered on the floor.

I've lost the will
To pick up the pieces alone,

Instead I just sit and wait
Gazing at the colors of our past.

"Saying Goodbye"
We smile over silky memories
That slide along our conversation.

We share stories and laugh.
Hearing him is like listening
To my own heart.

Spending time with him again
Is like the sun spilling onto my skin.
I forgot how warm and comforting it felt.

I am reminded at how connected we were:
Two trees with tangled roots.

We walk out of the restaurant,
Full of food and conversation.
I flood with emotion and hug him.

We linger in the hug
Letting the moment sink in.
He puts his arm around me and I follow.

We walk to our place of parting
And hug again, casually saying goodbye.
It's all we can manage.

We let our tangled roots and tongues
Speak for themselves.

"Stained Glass"
I haven't glued the pieces together.
I've placed them in a glass jar
To remember and smile
At the beauty that was.

I know they'll stay fragments,
Pieces of broken dreams:
Colorful wishes.

"For You to Know"
The person who left you
Seems so distant.

I feel about to burst from my seams;
I've dragged my shadow too long.

I let my face hang like a storm cloud, brooding.
No more, I'm pulling in the sunshine.

The person who left you
Clung to shards of broken glass.

The person who left you
Cried for milky memories thick with joy.

The person who left you
Let go like a rock sliding along a stream.

The person who left you
Seems so distant.

I've patched my heart with passion,
With dreams that spray across the sky.

I've fixed my heart to the earth
So it can't be blown away.

"Moment"
I'm an iceberg
Floating in the bitter cold.

I'm stone praying
To be chiseled.

I'm a sock
Lying without its mate.

I'm a bird
Who sings to no one.

I'm glass
Trying to be a wall.

I'm a puddle
Hoping to be a rainbow.

I'm a box of memories
Wishing I could hide inside.

I'm a fool
Trying to catch the fog.

I'm a flower
Trying to reclaim its roots.

"An Absent Memory"
I sink into softness:
that silk of silence
where my memories
stage their stories.

What had felt empty
now feels full,
but only of loneliness
and longing.

My mind is weighted
with the heaviness of my tears
as they threaten to tumble
to tell me it's true--

that I have held happiness,
clutched it,
and my hands still bleed
from the first time I said goodbye.

"My Winter in Teaching"
Slogging through the slush,
Tentatively stepping on the snow,
Trying not to cause a crisp crunch
To sever the serenity.

Staring at a mountain of snow
Wondering where the joy is
I once had in this pristine pile;
I start to shovel.

Everyone hates the heavy load
But finds satisfaction in the snow.
Why can't I?

"Dark Tears"
Her trembling hands cradle her face
And form a pool for her tears.
Shakes rack her body
And her sorrow echoes off the walls.
Moonbeams spill in
But are only distorted by the dreary darkness.
Trees' slender arms slide in for comfort
But their tangled empty embrace cannot reach her.
She claws at the recesses of her mind
Trying to find the answers
To the questions she never understood.
The answers are lost amidst the voices
That taunt her, telling her what she cannot bear.
She tries to close them out with her sobs,
With the screaming in her head
But they continue to clack their cacophonous
crimes.
And she cries on
With the angel crying with her.

"Broken"
Twisted in the moonlight
The trees' knotted arms
Rock in the wind.

I stand, shaken in the thorny breeze
That pricks my skin.
My thoughts leak into the silence,
Form in the silence,
Shattering the darkness.

I hear them slide out of my broken and brittle lips
And I cry to hear my own raspy voice.
I snap my heart's lock, tear it out of me
And throw it, still pumping, to the sidewalk.
I wait to see it sink slowly to a deflated sack
And I crumble to my knees wishing
I could grab the words from the air
And pull them back into the silence of my mind.

The moon dips behind a tree
And the light filters through its branches.
I scrape myself off the sidewalk
And walk into the shadows.

My head bobs as on a string.
My heart is still a bloody pulp on the ground
As I curse my memories for hammering a hole
In my heart and flying through like a ghost.

"Thoughts in Silence"   *For MG*
All the things that made him who he is,
His hobbies, interests and eccentricities,
Seem so trivial until death.
Those small details that we often take for granted
In remembrance are the aspects of the person
We hold so close.

People mean so much to us
That death is an empty state,
Taking away something of great value to us.
Yet we are pushed to move forward,
To live without,
To make do with what life left us,

But it's not enough.
It's never enough.

What if all one wants to do is stand and remember,
To hold tight to time
And never approach the future without them?

Who holds the key to happiness?
Once I have it I want to grip it until I bleed.

Spring

In the spring moments in life we experience times of love, beauty, and hope. We can even rediscover ourselves, where life has a new meaning and perspective.

"Me, You, Us"
It was as though
I was an inequality.

It was as though
I was a ship that needed a harbor,

And one day
The first page was written,
But I had no idea where the story would go.
I didn't know what kind of story it was.

After lines filled the pages I realized
I was the protagonist,
Time was the antagonist,
And love was the conflict.

And what were you?
You were what kept me
Turning the pages.

"Not For Sale"
I don't know why someone didn't just grab you
While they could,
Like two women fighting over
A slinky shirt on the sales rack.

Now it's too late;
You're not for sale.
I've pulled all the tags-no returns!
You're all mine,
And I'm so damn lucky.

"Romance"
My life melted,
Softened into smooth caramel,
Blended into a blurry dream
Of sticky sweetness I wanted to savor.
I longed for this moment for years,
The fragile star framed in my palm,
Yet still afraid its glow would fade
And I would be alone again
With only a taste to tease my tongue.

"To Feel Lucky"

How can you not love how his hand
Cups your cheek,
Pulls you close and kisses you with intensity:
A passion that sparkles, then softens like savoring
the taste of sweetness?

How can you not love how he cradles you
In his arms,
Creating a secure sense of safety that soothes,
And sensual feeling that saturates?

How can you not love how he shares your love
Of just opening a window and breathing in nature,
How he also stops and listens, takes it in, settled?

How can you not love how he smiles,
Pulls you close and dances with you,
His eyes shimmering like the stars
And your feel like heaven is in your hand?

How can you not feel lucky?

"My Theories on Time"

Sometimes I think that Time has gone on holiday
That she enjoys her leisurely time alone
And has never been in love.

Sometimes I think that Time
Has an odd sense of irony
That she orchestrates meetings
When emotion threatens logic,

And yet sometimes I think Time
Was right all along
And saw far beyond me.

"I Promise"
As the moon and stars
Stretch their light
Across the evening sky
You and I stand

Alone in the soft darkness.
A warm kiss
Caresses my emotions
And renews the breath
It sweetly took away.

I rest my head on your shoulder.
I cannot look into your eyes
And let you see the tears I feel,
The love that slides steadily
Down my face.

You lift my head
And you know my tears:
"This isn't goodbye.
It's finally our beginning."

"To Keep Me Going"
Have you ever made up stories
To keep you going?

I have made up stories
To keep you real.

I have made up stories
To keep me strong.

Have you ever replayed memories
To relive them?

I have replayed memories
To make me smile.

I have replayed memories
To reassure me.

But I know one day
I won't need stories,
I won't need memories,
Because I'll have you.

"Renewing"
Peeling the sorrow
From my skin,
I expose the fleshy fruit
Of joy
I'd forgotten I had,
Its red passion
Bursting to flow.

I scrape off the layers
Of indifference
And apathy
That have sunk into
My pores.

I slide into the silkiness
Of purpose and
Find comfort in walking in
Productivity.

Soon I will look in the mirror
And smile again.

"Finding Myself Again"
I am steel.

I get back up
And keep going,
Like a boxer.

I am finding myself
In a mountain of music,
Writing, and conversations.

I am reclaiming pieces of me,
Like reclaiming land.

I am detaching myself
From what I know
In order to be an individual again.

I am trying to put back the pillar
That is me,
To find who I am alone again.

Eventually I will be able to give myself again,
But only when I have all of myself to give.

"Realization"
I had a dream about love once.
I was holding his hand.
I was being held.
I was given notes.
I gave back rubs.
We sat in silence while hot chocolate
Steamed out of Christmas mugs
In the middle of May.
I cried over a misplaced sock
After a string of disappointments
From him, my husband.
I yelled at the cat
Because my husband wasn't home for dinner
On time.
He kicked me in the middle of the night,
Dreaming he was a horse.
I bruised and cried.
I slept on the couch.
Love wasn't supposed to be
A tangled web of mixed extremes.
It was supposed to only be euphoric.
It was supposed to be affectionate.
I wasn't supposed to sleep as far away from him
As possible
Because I didn't want to be touched,
Because I was hot and the air was sticky.

I wasn't supposed to go to bed
Furious
Because of the quirk I had thought
Was endearing.
Love wasn't supposed to be this way.
I dreamt of love once.

"After"

I had stones over my eyes.
My hands were limp leather.
But one held my hand,
Filled it with warmth.
It was a voice so familiar,
Like strains of music
From my favorite song.
He spoke with tears
In his throat
And kissed my forehead,
As if trying to awaken
Our soft memories
In my mind.

"To Wonder"
How can you not savor the unknown
And wonder what secrets it holds,
Stars it hides, fallen from the sky
That hold dreams of the future?

How can you not sit and wonder
On a quiet winter night
Who the man will be who will complement you
Sliding easily into perfection?

How can you not sit and wonder when
His light will shadow your door
And enter light into your home
And fill it with tangled arms and tender kisses?

How can you not hope in what is yet to be?

"Time to Wake Up"
I know that
It won't happen
To me.

I am different.
I am better.
I am above it.

The sooner
I learn
This is false

The better.
We are all blades
Of grass.

I may be a shorter stalk.
But we all swish to and fro
On the whims of the wind.

"The Cup"
It brims with familiar faces,
The liquid ripples like a still lake,
Browns blend with blacks in a swirl of color,
Images ebb and flow.

The liquid conforms to, and is protected by,
The sturdy trunk of clay that curves into a gaping u.

I see the cup's liquid brushed by a breeze,
Forms a mini wave

And I am reminded of the pages of a book
Flipped with speed: rustle.
The wave slips off the rim and sweet melodies
Slide down my throat.

If I pour out the contents,
I pour out my life.

"My Relationships"
I have 10 dollars.
I put it in my jeans left front pocket.
I wear the jeans all day.
I do not spend the 10 dollars
But I know it's there,
A rectangular outline,
Flat and Tight against my skin.

I misplace the jeans.
I lose the 10 dollars.
Those were my favorite jeans.
I was going to pay back my Gram
With that 10 dollars.

Six months later I clean out my closet
And in my chest of drawers
I find my dusty jeans,
Strangled under a pile of clothes.
The 10 dollars feels crisp in my hand
As I pull it out of the slip of the pocket.

"Why Bother to Worry?"
I waste so many breaths:
I could have,
I should have,
I might have,
I will.

I could,
I should,
I might,
I will,
Roll into a fist
And punch at my mind.

I waste so many breaths
Defending my mind
From
I could,
I should,
I might,
I will.

It's a never-ending battle until

I get up
And Do.
  Then I am given
  An oxygen mask.

"Pride"

Bells clatter
As I enter the store.
I stomp my feet,
Snow melts into the rubber
Welcome mat.
I look up at two wooden counters
And I meet a man's gaze.
"Can I help you?"
"I want to rent skis."
He smiles,
"Well I can help with that; what size shoe are you?"
 "I'm not sure."

He approaches me, squats by me
With a metal foot plate in his hand.
"Put your foot on this."
I hate not knowing my foot size.
"8 ½, I'll go get what you need."
I stand,
Alone in the empty store: 'Incapable.'
"Okay, slide your foot in.
You tighten it with this knob."
I make myself feel better:
"Oh, these are different than my old boots;
They had all the buckles."
"Yeah this is easier."
I try not to seem like an amateur.
"I haven't skied in years."

I'm talking
To make myself feel better.
I'm talking
To someone who doesn't care,
But I forget this.
I'm not who you think I am.
I'm not in high school.

I still need to prove myself,
Even in the ski shop.

"My Spring of Teaching"
The tulips spring up boldly,
Pushing their way up out of the hard earth--
And I find I was tough enough too
Because I'm no longer a slip of green.
I stand straight with a splash of color.

I'm no longer afraid.
I soak in the sun
And inch higher—
Reaching the other tulips.

I see beauty in my own color now.
I no longer cower in the corner.
The other tulips look on at my growth
And I see that we make a rainbow.

Summer

The summer of our lives are filled with joy and
contentment: grateful for all life has to offer.

"Strolling"
I walk among
The thick thorny blackberries
For a mile
As grass licks
At my shoes.
I hear the whir
Of a plump mother bee
Suck nectar from blossoms
On branches that bow in awe
To the sheer cliff face
The tree's roots cling to.

"Sitting on the Summer Side"
Brush strokes on the water
Are a painted picture of shades
Of blue, blended with streaks
Of yellow melted into gold,
And flecked with glimmering white.
Shaking green fronds waver
In the wind and leaves drift
Into the reflection, distorting it.

"Beautiful Decline"
I never thought I'd love
The smell of decay.

I never thought I'd love
The sound of fragile brittleness,
The crunch of fading life.

I never thought I'd love
A foreboding nakedness.

I never thought I'd love to see brokenness,
A lack of warmth and protection.

I never thought I'd love
To see where everything is stripped away.

I never thought I'd love
The silence that sings of loss,
A bitter emptiness.

I never thought I'd love to see a slow death,
Where bursting color withers to only a dull rattle
And yet I love to be immersed in this crucial time

That is Fall.

"Winter Rain"
I love the scent of the rain,
How its fragrance fills the air: crisp and fresh
As it crackles in my nose.

I love the rhythm of the rain,
How it cradles me in its soothing dance
Covering life, resting, so that new life may be born.

"Another Dreary Day:
The Beginnings of Winter"
The Billowing Wind,
Shakes me to the core,
Chills me to the bone,
And propels me to some destination,
I know not where.

The Billowing Wind
Numbs my thoughts,
Focuses on the frigid air,
And then leaves me there
To unnerve someone else.

"My Landscape"
Shades of gray and
Shades of green
Are drawn against a pale blue canvas.
Rounded tops and
Jagged tops
Mold and Shape the Sky.

Shaved Mountains of Granite
Are Faces formed over Time
And Become Relics of History.

"Sunset"

Clouds meld into purple grays,
Mesh with brilliant blues.
Long puffs of white contrast
Sharp blacks on a sparkling lake.
The sun sets on a lake
Hiding in a cavern of two mountains,
A bright orange ball, petite against the landscape.
Its thick line of light shines across the water
Shades of orange fall around it,
Dissipating into dark hues.

"Childhood Memories"
Raindrops fall,
Shimmering crystals,
Pale blue jewels,
Splashing on hot
Pavement.

You puddle jump,
Sloshing in the murky
Water, in galoshes
And a yellow plastic
Rain jacket.

Giggles of glee
Escape your lips.
Thunder peals through the sky,
And lightning soon follows,
But your smile never leaves.

Spinning in circles
The jewels drip down
Your face.
You taste the raindrops;
They melt in your mouth.

Ah the joy of playing
In the rain.

"Words,"
They pop like seeds
Onto the page.

They wade into my thoughts,
Weighted like stones,
And sink into my smile.

They are pebbles
Spilling off a spoon,
Clinking into existence.

They surround me like sunshine,
Envelope me like the wind,
And spring to life like daffodils.

"Inspiration"
I pull to the surface
The moments that drift in the depths
That is myself.

They linger and sink
Emotion filled, like being immersed
In water.

It's a surprise to see them pop up
Like silver and golden fish,
Darts of color in the vanilla canvas.

I cling to these times,
Like holds in a rock's shape
Moments of clarity in the murky purpose of life.

"In the Present"
I run to catch happiness
But I should be standing still.

I pull at the threads of future
Instead of weaving myself into the present.

In the silent solace of my thoughts
When I relinquish control, then I am here.

No Worries.

"Cosmos"   *For MG*
Pinpricks woven together
With black thread,
Gashes in the sky
Spaced apart, distant,
But always the thick black fabric
Binds them.

The black blends to gray and blue.
The pinpricks disappear,
Dissolve into the light,
Yet under the garment
Of wispy whites and swirling blues
Still that black thread,
Still that thick black fabric.

"The Rose"   *For EJW*

I see a glitter in her eyes.
It peers out from beneath her lashes;
It warms my soul.

Her feathery lips
Pout and smile;
Lines of poetry
Pour from them.

I see lines on her forehead
Crinkle like old parchment
And deepen
Like etched stone.

I rest my head against her shoulder
A rock, an anchor.
She reaches her right hand to touch my head,
Smoothes my hair and I close my eyes, grateful.

I am cradled,
A precious white rose, held in her ink stained
hands.
A petal will not fall
To the earth; it will not whither and brown.
It will open to full bloom.

"Dreams Can Become Reality"   *For AAM*
Words flow
Like black ink
Drifting into chains
Of soft moving lines.

Images rise and fall
Like the chest of a lover
As you rest your head
On his smooth skin,
And you feel his firm arms
Wrap you in a blanket
Of warmth.

Your eyes flutter
Like butterfly wings
And close like a trailing word's end.

Your mind swims in a sea of
Dreams with visions of sand
Sifting through your fingertips
As the sun soaks your bronzed skin.

Your eyes peruse
The rolling water for him.
You see a sea foam green sail
And your eyes glitter with the shimmer
Of your smile.

A hardcover copy of Shakespeare's works
Rests at your right hand
With dog-eared pages
And black lined passages.

Getting up, you brush off
Your white ribbed cotton tank top
And your pale blue shorts
For remnants of sparkling brown dust.

It's off to "Jewels of the Seaside,"
Your collectible store,
And not a tacky tourist shop.

You wave to his figure
That you can't see
And trudge through the sand,
Hot like a griddle.

Later, with a jolt you awaken,
Feeling his strong arms
Squeeze gently,
A protective reflex to keep you close.

He smiles lazily with groggy eyes
And releases your slender frame.
You lie on your side facing him,
And he rolls you over him
With a playfulness dancing in his eyes,

A smirk on his lips.
Electric attraction flows between you

As you pull him close
With your arm around his neck.
A soft and passionate kiss
Enflames both your bodies
As waves rush and break
Outside the bedroom window.

"Dream Catcher: Take 1"   *For AAM*

Ambitions and hopes rest on her eyelashes,
Transfer to her dreams as her eyes close to light
And embrace the darkness.
 In this fantastical world,
Her intense and intimate desires are realized
Each night on a blank movie screen.
And when her eyes flutter open in the morning,
Like a butterfly's wings, a smile grazes her rosy lips.
Her feet swing over to touch the floor
And they firmly plant themselves
As she stands and stretches, yawning,
Greeting the day with open arms.

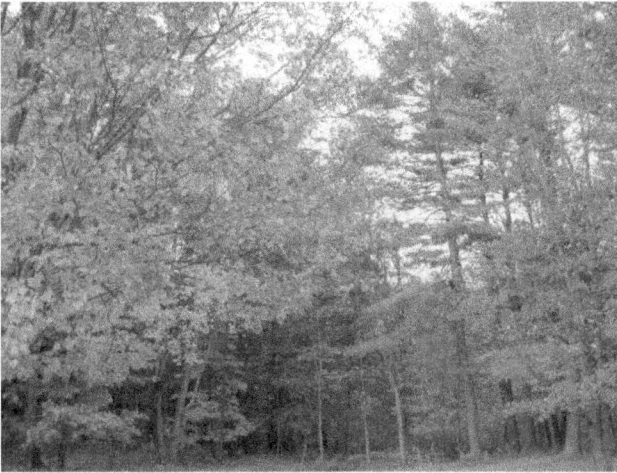

Fall

Sometimes we have a bit of fall in us: times in our lives
when we feel lost or discouraged.

We need to remember the beauty in our lives, the burst
of potential like the colors of fall.

"Never Original"

"Rated, dated, dater, rates, crates..."
"Got it, got it, that one too, cross it out,"
I hear in reply to my words.
Slowly the letters begin to disappear under
A line of ink and my family racks up the points.
"Katie," Dad asks as he goes around the table.
"I got 2." He repeats the number aloud
And records it,
"Weasie," he calls to my mom.
 She answers, "24."
I cross out my own score tally and box my words in
For another round of listing words someone else
Already has.

"All Those December 25ths
 Blacked Out on my Calendar"   *For EJW*
Ribbons are twisted and ripped,
Caught in a tangled mess,
No longer part of the Christmas wrapping paper
Like the gift it once was attached to.
No, it's just the remnants of love left behind,
Of well-meant thoughts blown out the window
With the chilled winter wind and silent snowdrifts.

All these presents are now just in pieces of ribbon.
They might as well be shards of glass for me
To pick up and throw away,
In that plastic garbage bag
That has a suffocation warning.

It used to be all glitter, shine, and color,
But now it's only dull empty sockets
That look at me in the mirror
And I see all the Christmases have left me.
I have nothing left to hope for,
Nothing left to hang on to,
Only the finishing touches to a present.

Until I see the twinkle of white Christmas tree
Lights in his eyes
And I wonder if he can brighten my holidays again,
And untangle my mess of ribbons,
And the presents left behind.

"All Consuming Vows"   *For MG*
It was as if time fragments
Had slipped through her colander,
Got sucked up by her vacuum,
Blended with her infant's cry
And enveloped by her husband's presence.
And in the end she couldn't figure out
Where those time fragments had gone
And why there was no time left
For her.

"Seeking God"   *For TC*
Wandering through an endless valley,
Running down a dead end alley,
Wondering when the escape will come,
And the tangled nerves will come undone,
It doesn't seem fair
And answers come so rare.

Lord I don't know why I'm here
Or if I'm even near
The place you want me to be,
But I'm trying to squint and see
This is my plea:
Guide and Protect me.

I don't understand.
Please take my hand.
I feel so alone
And my thoughts always roam
To doubts and self hate
Is it too late?

To start anew
And live in You?

"Outlook Over the Next Year"
The road stretches before me
Like tire spikes:

A long line of injuries
Stepping around obstacles,
Stepping around the pain.

The year stretches before me
Like a rubber band about to snap:

Taut talks about tense situations
And I want to scream and run away,
But I'm banging my head against too many walls.

Time stretches before me
Like drips from an IV:

Every day filled with essential activities
I don't have energy to do
Because worry and stress are fighting it out
In my head.

Every conversation I have is
Like an empty glass:

I have no one to fill it
With the hope and satisfaction I crave.

The road stretches before me.
The year stretches before me.
Time stretches before me.

Now sit there and tell me
It's easy or be strong,
And that's there's some big plan in all this.

You tell me that - and all these words will smack
you.

"Between Places"
I tug at my memories,
Pulling them into the present,
But they resist.

I push at my present,
Coaxing it towards the future,
But it stands fast.

I'm stuck in world of half me's,
Where each one laughs
Because they won't form a whole.

I try to find my appreciation
In a layer of mist but only parts emerge
From the dense clouds and I grab the pieces.

I look for understanding and strength
In the mess of papers and feelings in my room,
But I just find tears.

I listen for answers in the music of the crickets,
And the hum of the wind,
Only blankness.

Alone in my uncertainty.
Fragmented in heart and body.
I reach for my jar of hope and find it empty.

"Finding Peace and Pieces of Me"
Drops of sunshine sprinkle into my life,
Moments of clarity.

The drops dry, uncollected,
And I wonder why I'm unsatisfied.

That note, that phone call, that smile
Drift like wisps of smoke and fade: undone.

I beat on my soul until it's bloody with guilt,
Yet I apply band-aids and whisper to myself
reasons.

When will I be who I admire,
        Instead of playing dress up?

"The Struggle"
Tangled thoughts
Are threads that bind my mind.

I fumble in the clutter of the closets of my mind,
Searching for answers: dust and debris.

I gaze at the memories in broken frames.
Can they tell me how to proceed? Can they tell me
why I'm here?

Choking on words that stick in my throat,
Words that splinter: useless.

I gasp and gulp moments from the sea,
Emerging full of emotion. I push myself back down
to drown.

Why?

How do I make smooth my knotted life?
How do I stay a river of love and keep my shape?
How do I speak and not swallow stones of regret?

I close my eyes.

I pray.

"Moments"
Drag their leaded feet
Along my wooden floor,
Clanking, and scratching,
With pitted eyes they grope at the boards.

I wish they'd unchain themselves.

Moments flicker like candles,
Sparkle and disappear and I watch them go,
Clinging to their vibrancy,
Wishing they'd burn forever.

I wish the moments stuck in the sky like the sun.

Sitting, molding the couch,
Timing my life by a stop watch,
I'm moving so slowly,
Wishing I wasn't mush.

I wish I was a stone rolling down a hill.

It'd be so much easier if my mind
Wasn't weighted by anchors,
Clogged by marbles clacking together,
Full of fluff, wondering,

Which moments matter?
I think my answer would be: All of them.

"Finding My Place"
My eyes slid silent
In hopes that I would find answers
To the weighted questions that fell fast
Down my cheeks.

I embraced the blackness,
Because its emptiness was tangible.
Not because I found solace
In its lost loneliness,
But because at least I could dream
Of light.

www.ingramcontent.com/pod-product-compliance
Lightning Source LLC
Chambersburg PA
CBHW021218020426
42331CB00003B/363